THE PASSING SHOW: FIVE MODERN PLAYS IN VERSE

Published @ 2017 Trieste Publishing Pty Ltd

ISBN 9780649501786

The Passing Show: Five Modern Plays in Verse by Harriet Monroe

Edited by Trieste Publishing Pty Ltd.
Cover @ 2017

www.triestepublishing.com

HARRIET MONROE

THE PASSING SHOW: FIVE MODERN PLAYS IN VERSE

Trieste

The Passing Show

Five Modern Plays in Verse

By Harriet Monroe

BOSTON and *NEW YORK*
Houghton, Mifflin and Company
The Riverside Press, Cambridge
1903

Published November 1903

Go, book of me, to the one who knows —
If one there be.
Yea, bear me where that spirit goes,
And set me free.

CONTENTS

THE THUNDERSTORM

A Play in Two Acts

PERSONS OF THE PLAY.

John Mather.

Adela Mather, his wife.

Stephen Mather, his brother.

Dexter Dalton.

Laura Dalton, wife to Dexter.

Felix Merivale.

Lois Dale.

The action takes place at the country house of John Mather, during a summer afternoon and evening.

The Thunderstorm

Act I.

Scene. — *The large living-room of a suburban house, with a broad screen door and windows opening on a roofed veranda.* Lois Dale, *at the window, is watching the heavy rain, while* Stephen Mather *listlessly fumbles magazines on the table. Time, late afternoon.*

Lois. The rain would drown the summer if it dared,
Deep in a thick gray sea.
Stephen. It pours like mad.
Lois. See the whipt trees praying for mercy!
Stephen. Yes —
A nice time, this, to ask a crowd from town!
Lois. Do you remember —
Stephen. What?

Lois. Those lovely lines —
That poem of your brother's which has made
The lost world sing forever to the rain?
Stephen. Remember? — No! — John and his poetry!
Lois. How will you answer the avenging gods
For such contempt?
Stephen. The gods will take my part.
A man should play his rôle.
Lois. And if your brother
Were born to be a poet? —
Stephen. He would be one,
Instead of making steel.
Lois. Of course — how simple
A thing it is to live!
Stephen. Genius will out.
Lois. If all the happy stars conspire. If not,
Who can persuade the stars?
Stephen. Has he done nothing?
Steel is the better for him.
Lois. Yes, and so
You will not loose your hold. If he were born
For singing, and this yoke upon his neck
Were bound by all the indissoluble ties!
Your father dying then, his brave career
To be fulfilled; your mother, sisters, you

To serve! Ah, could a poet be a man,
Loving and living, and deny these claims?
But now —
Stephen. And you would solemnly convince me
That he should drop the mills and give himself
Forever to the muse!
Lois. Give him himself.
I care not whether he make steel or verses,
So he be free.
Stephen. Pshaw! — you are crazy too.
'T is merely madness with him, mere excess;
One of his ways of rioting. Who knows
What new fantastic license he may take
When the wild mood is on?
Lois. What happens when
The steam that ought to turn a thousand wheels
Finds its vent closed?
Stephen. What a fine tragedy
You build us out of common clay like ours,
Here in the suburbs!
Lois. Tragedy should dwell
In mediæval palaces afar,
Trailing her purple robes!
Stephen. Perhaps it 's you
Who are the poet.

Lois. If it were — alas! —
Rather this tempest beating on my head
Than to be housed in here!

Enter Laura Dalton.

Laura. What's to be done?
No golf, no riding, nothing in the world —
But —

Stephen. Talk to me.

Laura. Who could ask more than that?
Where's John?

Stephen. So — always John. What do you want
With John?

Laura. To be amused.

Stephen. Will no one ask
My gifted brother for a moon or two?
He has a special line of moons.

Laura. The sun will do —
A little sunshine.

[Lois *goes through the screen door and walks up and down on the broad roofed veranda, watching the rain; then sits down out of sight.*

Stephen. Lois tires of us.

Laura. No wonder!

Stephen. Does your ladyship intend
A compliment?

Laura. With you in such a temper,
Why should she stay?
Stephen. With you seeking another,
Should I be gay?
Laura. Oh, you are wearisome.
Stephen. If so to you, what am I to myself?
Laura. A god, I half suspect.
Stephen. Since I adore
A goddess?
Laura. Go adore some human girl,
And marry her, my boy, and so be sure
To have one worshiper forever.
Stephen. Sure! —
Of any woman?
Laura. Oh, how cynical!
How most profoundly wise!
Stephen. And if I have
A cynic's wisdom, many thanks to you,
Who teach me day by day.
Laura. Poor sufferer!
Have I not sins enough, and heavy enough
That you should burden me with yours?
Stephen. One sin
You have — you like to watch me in the cage.
But some fine day I'll break it.
Laura. And be free?
Nothing would please me more.

Stephen. Yes, it would please you
To feel my claws at last.

Laura. And recognize
At last the animal.

Stephen. You guileless women —
With your conventional morality!
What would become of all your principles
In any more indecorous land or age
Than this, I wonder?

Laura. So — are these your claws
I do not like them.

Stephen. Hm! this is a growl —
No more.

Laura. Why should I listen to your growls?

[*She takes a book from the table and sits down to read. He walks up and down. A pause.*

Stephen. It rains.

Laura. Ah — does it?

Stephen. Once upon a time
There was a deluge.

Laura. Really!

Stephen. Your book
Is quite absorbing.

Laura (*yawning*). Yes — "Degeneration,"
The cheerful German outlook.

Stephen. It is queer
How many pages some men will consume
To show what fools they are.
Laura. And other men
Must prove it in their deeds.
Stephen. Yes, but with us
The truth is not blazoned before the world;
It lies between one woman and oneself.
Laura. Not always.
Stephen. Do you mean —
Laura. Oh yes, I mean
Only last night my husband laughed at you.
Stephen. Damn him!
Laura. What would you do, I wonder now,
In any world less decorous than this?
Stephen. Kill, I suppose.
Laura. And here you can do nothing
But make yourself ridiculous.
Stephen. Take care —
You go too far.
Laura. Oh, let me read.
Enter Dexter Dalton *and* Felix Merivale.
Dalton. Not here!
He must be drowned, I think. Laura, wake up.
What shall we do to-night to outwit the storm?
Laura. Give it its will.

Dalton. I fancy we shall have to
There, out-of-doors. But here, under this roof —
Come, let us challenge it.
Laura. Do — what to do? —
As though one could be merry by design!
Merivale. A vaudeville!
Dalton. This literary juggler
Will toss a novel, essay, play, and poem
All in the air at once.
Merivale. This connoisseur
Of law and art will make miraculous leaps
Upon the double trapeze.
Laura (*pointing to* Stephen). And there is one
Who at a wink will swallow swords of fire.
Stephen. If you provide them.
Dalton. And the lady there
Shall wield the whip and keep us in the ring.
Laura. The ladle, do you mean?
Merivale. Ah, you have heard
The story of —
Stephen. Of course we have.
Merivale. The story —
Dalton. Which is it? Who will guess?
Merivale. A new one, friends;
And apropos — about a punch-bowl.

Stephen. New!
As though he could for even a single day
Keep a new tale unprinted!
Merivale. And if not
'T is you, my unappreciative friends
Who are to blame. You force me to appeal
To the wise public.
Stephen. Happy public!
Laura. Come —
Tell me the tale. I am extremely wise,
And sympathetic as a summer breeze.
Stephen. Beware!
Laura. Tell me the tale.
[Laura *and* Merivale *sit down in a corner to talk.* Dalton *has been examining a landscape on the wall.*
Dalton. Ah, what a touch!
Where did John dig up this Cézanne?
Stephen. In Rouen.
Some little local dealer did n't know
What he had got and sold it for a song.
You like it?
Dalton. It 's a gem. What modeling!
The very pulse-beat of the sun! It 's queer
What that old vagabond divined before
Monet put brush to canvas. See that sky —

Brazen, relentless, dreaming of a storm!
I have seen skies like that.

Stephen. Have you, indeed?
I doubt if Cézanne ever did.

Dalton. But look —
He painted it.

Stephen. Ah, did he? I hate pictures,
Damn them at random, don't pretend to know;
But John adores that medley just because
The painter stopped halfway. Your brazen sky
Is the bare canvas.

Dalton (*confused*). On my soul, it is!
Just like Cézanne.

Stephen (*lighting a cigarette*). To trip his worshipers?
Alas, these connoisseurs! Why not admit
That you and I don't know a thing about it?

Dalton. This light, you know — the storm —

Stephen. Ah, yes — I know —
It is the light, of course.

Laura (*looking around*). Tell me the quarrel.
What are these gibes?

Stephen. Nothing — we were admiring
Cézanne's relentless sky.

Laura. Look out, my jewel.
I always said this sudden zeal for art
Would get you into trouble.

Dalton. Look at her!
Impeach my connoisseurship, if you dare,
Before *that* picture. She refutes the slander,
And makes me proof against the jeering world
And all the freaks of genius.

Stephen. Yes, I knew
She could work miracles.

Dalton. Come, Merivale,
And help me down this Philistine.

Merivale. Young David
Suing for help! The rain has spoiled my weapons —
I am as sluggish as a crocodile.

Laura. We are a stagnant pool. Yet if some hand
Should throw a single stone into its depths —

Stephen. What hand?

Merivale. What stone?

Laura. Anyone! anything!
Oh, I am tired of sitting on the rim
And staring at my inner consciousness.

Merivale. Where is Miss Dale? Ask her to throw the stone.

Stephen (*contemptuously*). Lois!

Enter Adela Mather.

Adela. Where is she? Yes, and John is gone.
I have been looking for him everywhere.

Stephen. Portentous!

Adela. He's not here — not in the house.

Laura (*rising abruptly*). But she is!

Adela. Where?

Laura. She was — where did she go?

Adela. Well, where?

Stephen. Don't be alarmed — she's on the porch.

Why are you always rushing here and there,
And doing this and that?

Adela. How can I help it,
Married to him?

Stephen. Let him alone! Good heaven!
Send him to China, or the pyramids,
And see if this unconscionable world
Can get along without him.

Merivale. There are others.

Stephen. Perhaps.

Merivale. Well, we shall see.

[*Exit* Merivale *to the porch.*

Adela. If I could know
Just once what he would do that very minute,
I might have hopes of ease.

Stephen. You never will.

Adela. I must. Oh, for a husband like the rest,

Who travels in the road and does not wander
Through every sunny field!
Laura. Faith, what a wish! —
A husband like the rest!
Dalton. Faith, what a slur!
See how they love us, Mather, — these our wives;
And then go find one.
Stephen. He who puts his trust
Upon a woman —
Laura. Is a Solomon
Compared with her who pins her faith upon
A man.
Adela. They are such infants, and of all
The children who blow bubbles in the sun,
John is the willfulest.
Laura. Then give him up,
And let him blow his bubbles. After all,
They shine.
Stephen. And burst.
Laura. Well, most things do — alas!
So why not sparkle if you can, before
The suffocating tragedy?
Adela. Meantime
I shall go mad of sheer bewilderment.
My brain is tired with following him, with trying

To think ahead of him.

Stephen. The brains of women
Were never made to think. 'T is not alone
Yourselves you tire by thinking.

Laura. Thought is slow,
Roundabout — masculine, in short. But we —
We know without it.

Stephen. Far too well.

Adela. Then tell me —
How does it stand with Lois? Will she take him? —
For I can neither think nor do I know.

Laura. Well, Merivale is famous, rich enough,
And most persistent —

Stephen. And a poet, too —

Laura. The people's own. And Lois —

Stephen. And our Lois
Is thirty-one.

Adela. What does she care for that?

Laura. What you or I or any woman cares.
And yet —

Adela. Well —

Laura. Yet I dare not say she 'll do it.

Stephen. Then she 's a fool.

Laura. Yes — doubtless. Women are
Frequently fools.

Adela. If she should let him go
She would deserve all the hard knocks and more
That fate has given her.

Laura. Yes — poor girl — deserve
To play at odds with life till death comes by
And pities her.

Enter Lois *and* Merivale *from the porch.*

Lois. I fear for you.

Merivale. Alas —
Throttle your conscience.

Lois. Novels rushing out
From the hot press in legions, editors
Clamorous for a line, three plays at once
Crowding three houses, critics on their knees —

Merivale. Well, since they would not take my best — alas! —
I had to do my worst.

Lois. The grateful people!
How richly they reward the lucky man
Who gives them what they want! come, friends and foes,
What shall we do to dim his lucky star
And save this laureled victor from success?

Merivale. Is she not kind?

Lois. Success the sycophant,
Whose smile hides treachery, who fawns and serves

That so man may forget and be her slave;
Success, who holds his weakness then by threats
And whispered fears; who hides the truth from
him
And the stern front of justice, and at last
When she has won him wholly, till his soul
Is mirrored in her eyes, casts him away
To all the dogs of ruin.

Laura. To your knees,
And pray the gods for failure.

Merivale. I am saved.
Success may do her worst — it is not much,
While this philosopher despises her.

Dalton. She 's not so bad — I think that even
to-day
If she should offer me her poisoned cup
I 'd drink it to the dregs.

Stephen. And ask for more.

Lois. Yes, that 's the way with us. And so
even you,
With million-dollar cases in your office
And masters' masterpieces on your walls —
Even you have not enough.

Dalton. No — not enough.
These million-dollar cases in the courts,
That stay there with their millions; and these
pictures,

That hide their secrets from the rich and great
To tell them unto babes! Ah, do not fear!
Success? — there's no such thing!

[John Mather, *who has entered the house unperceived from the other side, in riding dress, and thrown off a wet cape and hat in the hall, now walks in quietly. His top-boots and trousers are splashed with mud and rain.*

John. Despise it then.
Dalton. Well, you're a spectacle!
Laura. God of the storm!
Adela. O John, what have you done?
Lois. Blown with the gale!
What did the thunder say?
John. It said — ride fast,
And loose the world like me!
Stephen. Fine day for riding.
John. Glorious! for ten thousand shining demons
Joined in the race, slapping their saucy sides.
Laura. And did you beat them?
John. Else how am I here?
Look — the storm nods; the rain falls sullenly,
Heavy and straight and languid. But at first

The fallen gods crossed swords with gods of light
For a lost world.

Lois. Which side had your allegiance?

John (*smiling*). My friend the devil deserves my loyalty.
Has he not played me fair?

Adela (*who has hurried out and returned with a glass of whiskey-and-water*). Here, John, drink this.
You'll take your death.

John. Death would be sweet to take —
A green place by the dusty road, a pause,
A silence. Speak no ill of death! But this —
Pale counterfeit of life! Give it to Dalton,
And help him change the color of his world.

Dalton (*taking it*). If ever a color needed changing —

Laura. Yes —
We have been gray — ashes and mud and lead.
Show us the gold.

Stephen. Being a poet.

John. Ah —
Who told you?

Stephen. Lois tells me that the muses
Wear mourning for you.

John. Lois knows them.
Lois. Hush!
I dream of them, but in their sacred groves
You walk anointed.
John. Then, by all the gods,
This day we climb Olympus. Let us have
Revels to match the tempest, set our feast
Above these quarreling clouds, and for a night
Make the immortals envious!
Lois. What are we —
To brave the gods!
Laura. Immortals, too! The word
Is given — I feel the aureole 'round my hair.
Stephen. Beware! — the earth's a comfortable place.
Dalton. But tiresome, though. Let's try the other sphere!
Merivale. Myself have had some commerce with the gods —
John. And found them docile, did you? You shall be
Apollo, with the morning in your eyes.
Merivale. A pretty tribute to my beauty!
Lois. Yes —
And talents manifold.
Laura. And I —

John (*bowing low*). And you —
Who else but Aphrodite?
Stephen. By that token,
I will be Mars.
Dalton. A proper rôle!
Lois. Nay, Jove —
Ruler of gods and men.
John. Yea, so he is;
Jove of the cheque-book, the great modern god,
Who keeps us groveling mortals at our work.
Stephen. Poor Jupiter, whom all obey and fear!
If I am he, who may not be beloved,
Beware my lightnings!
Adela. Who am I then?
Laura. Juno —
The queen of heaven and mistress of the world.
Adela. A pack of empty titles!
Lois (*to* John). Piteous,
Tragic beyond the cunning of the fates,
Is each new comedy you choose to play.
John. Then play it to the death!
Lois. I cannot hear
Your words for voices, nor can see you there
For ghosts that rise.
John. Defy them! — if you don't

They strangle you. Behold her — she is Pallas,
With wisdom on her lips —
Lois. And pain at heart.
John. Would you be wise and happy both? Not here,
Not even on high Olympus may you brave
The envy of the gods. Hear me once more!
The word goes forth that may not be recalled.
Dalton is Hermes — Hermes the quick-witted,
Light-footed, and light-fingered.
Dalton. Ha! — and you?
John. And I am Bacchus — he has whispered me! —
Bacchus, the god of revels. If I know him,
He is the only sane one at the feast;
He, sad with too much joy, and heavy-witted
With too much knowledge, who alone of all
At loaded tables may forbear — behold,
I place his chaplet on my brow, and now
Summon you in his name. When the clock grows
Fat with big hours, meet me and have your will,
Immortals all!
Laura. To hear is to obey.
John. Go and prepare your souls — each one alone.
Lose the dark world —

Adela. But, John, it 's dinner-time.
John. He dines who will — I fast before the feast.
Dreams are the meat to feed on when the earth
Sinks like a stone, the meat to make us bold
Among the stars, our peers.
Lois. To make us mad.
John. And if there 's joy in madness —
Merivale. Let us go!
Dreams or a dinner — there 's the choice.
Stephen. I choose
What I am sure of.
Laura. There thou liest! Nay,
What he is never sure of does man choose —
'T is Aphrodite speaks.
Merivale. And Jupiter,
Who hates the truth like other crownèd kings
Heeds not the blasphemy.
Dalton. The word is given.
Away — each to communion with his soul!
Stephen. Or stomach.
Adela. Heavens! what next!
Lois. The word is given.
When the black hours grow big —
John. When each has won
His secret from the silence, come again.

(CURTAIN.)

ACT II.

SCENE.— *The dining-room, with a round mahogany table set as at the end of a supper. A screen-door, at right, opens on the veranda. It is after midnight. The supper is over, but the people are toying with nuts, candies, wine-glasses, etc., and plenty of champagne is cooling on the buffet. Some of the party are drawn up to the table, others have left it, others recline classically on couches. They wear costumes ridiculously significant of the gods whose characters they assume, or of the modern import of those gods; such draperies and emblems as they could make up impromptu from the resources of the house and garden, and wear or carry, usually over their ordinary dress.* JOHN, *as Bacchus, has the head of the table, with* LAURA, *as Aphrodite, in a costume charming but rather daring, at his right. His wife, as Juno, reclines on a couch opposite him, with* MERIVALE, *as Apollo, and* LOIS, *as Pallas, near her.* STEPHEN, *as Zeus, reclines lazily at the rear, with* DALTON, *as Hermes, beside him.*

John. Now ye have feasted, fill your cups again!
We feed on things that perish, and from them
Take the immortal essence, and so dare
To know whither and whence, and bear unwearied
The burden of the suns. Lift the wine high,
And tell us, with its nectar on your lips,
Your errand in a sacrilegious world
That would forget the gods. What make ye here,
Banished long since in shame? Great Jove the king,
What mak'st thou here?

Stephen. Since I am Jove the king,
Why should I talk? Deeds are my line, not words.
My only voice is thunder.

Laura. Dost thou find
The hearts of mortals changed?

Stephen. How should I know,
Who never think? I'm running railroads now
And drawing cheques. The world was but a garden
When I was young — now it's a factory.
Well, it is easier to handle so,

With all mankind going the self-same way,
Doing the self-same thing.

Laura. And yet to me
'T is the same wanton world. Now as of old
Men make a great ado of business —
War, trade, and tyranny — yet now, as then,
They live and die for love.

John. Hush! dost thou dare
Utter the secret word? Banish the thought
From our chaste company, lest it should bring
Madness more rash than sparkles in this wine.
Athene, from thy deeps beyond calm eyes
Teach her the joys of wisdom.

Lois. Ignorant
Thou art, to deem that joy is wisdom's quest.
Serene she is and selfless her desire.
Beyond the lowly haunts of joy and sorrow
She ranges with the stars.

Laura. And so on earth
Has little influence.

John. And so on earth
Has more than we, showing the way to spurn it,
And thus be free. She is the enemy —
None but her do I fear. For all ye others

This drug has sleep or madness. Drink it down,
And let Apollo soothe us with a song.
Tune up, sweet brother, or thy muses nine
I 'll fuddle one by one.

[*They drink, all but* John *and* Lois, *who merely touch their glasses.* Merivale *rises, strikes his banjo, and chants his song to its accompaniment.*

Adela (*to* Dalton). What fools we are!

Dalton. Can't help it, I suppose;—it 's in the air.

Merivale.

I am Apollo, who of yore in groves abided
With maidens nine to hark enchanted to my song.
I am Apollo, who upon the sun resided,
Driving through heaven the fiery coursers all day long.
To me came embassies from suppliant states in sorrow,
To me came hearts at war and fearful of their doom;
For out of yesterday I dragged the shy to-morrow,
And lo, her eyes avowed their rapture and their gloom.

But to-day 't is a different rôle
  That the tired world bids me play;
I who chanted of old to its soul
  Must amuse the poor world to-day.
So I hint at a thousand loves
  In a delicate medley of rhymes,
And I thrill when the spirit moves
  Over popular wars and crimes.
But who cares what I sing to my lyre?
It is lost in the roaring of fire,
For in clamorous towns I dwell
Near the steel-forged gates of hell.

John. A toast — Apollo, though his voice be lost,
His seven strings snapped!

All. Apollo!

[*They rise and drink the toast, as before.*

Merivale. Sweet immortals,
As I am modest, turn your favor from me.
Why should I speak when Juno, queen of heaven,
Is silent?

Adela. Do not vex your soul for her.
Juno was always out of it, poor thing! —
Poor fool!

Stephen. Great Sister, consort of my state,
What brings thee earthward now?

Adela. I do not know.
Did Juno ever know?
Dalton. Juno is here
To guard her interests; — that 's my business too.
But mine have multiplied since thieves became
So numerous, the tricks of trade so deep.
Wings are not swift enough — I need to-day
Railroads, the telegraph, the telephone;
And even then, so dull are grown the gods,
These men outwit me.
John. Hermes, god of trusts,
Of strikes and lock-outs and combines. At last
We have no need of Mars — look, he is banished;
For nimble Mercury, the unscrupulous,
Is the great modern god of war.
Dalton. Ah, yes.
Mars cut a dash at first — the blusterer! —
But I have undermined his credit, even
Married his sweetheart, you observe.
Laura. He 's rich,
A good provider — how could I resist him,
Who need so much of late — such palaces,
And gowns?
Merivale. Since he has grown so powerful,
A toast!

Him let Apollo praise
  Who 'll pay for singing!
When withered are the bays
  And love 's a-winging,
Money is good as new —
  It fails us never.
Give to the giver his due —
  Hermes forever!

John (*to* Laura). Behold how low the gods are fallen,
When even you, the queen of love and beauty,
Drink to the lord of lies.

Laura (*softly to* John). The queen of love! —
But if I may not speak my one great word,
What then is left but lies?

John (*aloud*). Thou shalt speak all. —
To-night all words are uttered.

Laura (*softly*). If thine ear,
Wherein my word would rest, will hear it not,
Then speech is but a lie.

John. Not mine alone!
If stars reveal their souls and have no fear,
Lo, shall we wear the world's hypocrisies,
We who beyond the stars may range at ease?

[*Standing, with brimming glass lifted.*

Drink — to the truth, for now the truth is ours,

Now we are gods. The truth! The veils are
torn,
The masks are buried with mortality,
And he who lies must do it to high heaven!
The truth! Vain is denial, vain — more vain
Is silence; yea, unutterably vain
The rags we wear to hide us from ourselves.
Thus to the light lift up your brimming souls
And let their secrets break upon your lips!
The truth!

[*They rise, and lift glasses high to accept the toast, saying:* —

Many voices. The truth!

Lois. Does moody Bacchus dare
Summon the truth — the god who maddens her
With wine, and smothers her with sleep, who
fears
To meet her level eyes?

John. Mad or asleep,
Then only doth she flee the bounds of sense
And shake her great wings free. The truth! —
she 's mine,
By all her dreams! mine, by the sudden lights
That flame her frenzied eyes! Think you to
find her,
Led by blind owls of learning? — I have hated

The owl since long ago he hooted me
In Nysa's groves. The truth — beware of her,
Lest her swift fires consume thee!
Lois. She is mine —
For love, not fear. She dwells in quietness
With wisdom, and the peering paths of science
Lead to her grove. My votaries are hers,
And they outrun swift Hermes with his wings,
Yea, rob Jove of his lightnings.
Stephen. Haughty maid,
Beware those lightnings! Truth is mine alone,
For power is mine, and truth is power.
Merivale. Nay, mine;
For what is truth till it be uttered? Mine,
By all the muses!
Laura. Words! vain, boastful words!
None of ye knows the truth.
John. In beauty alone —
Laura. Nay, not in beauty nor song nor power nor wisdom,
Nor yet in madness dwells the truth.
Stephen. Then where?
Laura. 'T is hence — ye have no power to summon it.
'T is with the absent god.
John. Drink to him then —
Challenge the absent god!

Laura. And dost thou dare?

John. Why not?

Laura. The insidious, vengeful, jealous god,
Who even on the immortals has no pity —
Invoke him not!

John. Great Eros, now to thee
We pour this golden wine. Bring us the truth —
Yea, though thou strip and scourge us, lash it home,
That we may know the utmost, dare the worst,
And so be free!

[*They drink, as before.*

All but Lois. Eros!

Merivale (*to* Lois). Your heart 's a-cold!
You will not drink to Eros — then beware
His vengeance!

Lois. What shall wisdom fear?

Merivale. To die
Of thirst at last.

Stephen. Immortals, will you take
This potion he has mixed to make us mad
And let him pass it by? No, by this lightning!
Down with it, Bacchus — do not sit and stare
While we sink deeper in your cups.

Dalton. Take heart —
'T is not so bad, this potion.

John. Bacchus gives
Freely his wild delights. Yea, all but he
May know the rapture, compass for an hour
The rounded heavens and mount their peaks
of fire;
While he, alone with dull satiety,
Must brood upon their bliss.
Laura. Who ever thought
Bacchus would grow so eloquent? Taste the
cup,
And with its magic on thy lips, thy song
Shall make Apollo envious.
Merivale. Try it then,
And take Apollo's laurels if thou canst!
John. The cold green leaves — keep them!
For me the fruit,
Heavy and rich and red!
Stephen. Down with it then!
Dost hear me? — I am Jove! Search thine
own truth
Even to the dregs. Drink, for the gods all
thirst
Till Bacchus drinks.
Laura. Soften your heart with wine,
That Aphrodite's word may sink as deep
As burning coals in snow.

John. What says she there,
That face of stone?
Lois. Nothing.
John. What thinks she there, —
She in whose thought we float like silver moons,
Lofty, a-cold. She doth despise too much.
Look, when I lift the glass how her eyes glare!
Laura. Bacchus! a toast! a toast! With brimming cups
We wait the magic word.
Dalton. A song! a song!
Tune up Apollo's lyre — I found it first.
'T is thine to-day.
John. Your hearts! give me your hearts,
And let them beat the music of my song.
(*He sings.*)

Fill full your deep goblets, immortals!
Dark red be the flood!
For we who would pass the dream portals
Must drink our heart's blood.
We must drink our heart's blood!

Red wine! with all life like a jewel
Dissolved in the cup —
Love, faith, yea, and glory the cruel —
Fill full, fill it up!
Fill it full, fill it up!

Give all! be it God or the other
 Who takes it at last!
Drink deep! 't is a sob that we smother,
 A die that is cast.
 'T is a die that is cast.

[*Led by* Stephen, *they laugh and lift glasses with nervous hilarity.*

Lois. Horrible! horrible!

Merivale. Oh, toss it off!
Laugh that you may not weep.

Lois. Weep — weep forever!
Let the world drown in tears!

John. What does she say?

Lois. This — that across your path I lay my sword:
You shall not drink that cup.

Adela. Shall not, indeed!

John. Your sword! is it not always in my way?

Laura. 'Forward! it is not dangerous.

Stephen. What folly!

Lois. Oh, for God's air! oh, for the sound of wings!
Here there are flames and creeping things. — Come out
Into the storm.

John. And then —

Lois. You cannot do it —
And sing your soul away. Do you not see
The pit there? Look — you will not.

Adela (*to* Lois). Who are you
To take command here? Let him have his way,
So 't is not yours!

Laura. Adela!

Adela (*to* Laura). You as well!
All, all these elbowing women! Give me room —
I suffocate.

Laura. Good God!

Adela. Mummers and masks!
Is it not clear as day, your pretty game?
I have a rôle to play.

[*During these speeches, the people drop partially their disguises, so far as they may be easily and instantly cast off.*

Stephen (*to* Laura). Have you had enough?
Is this the truth we drank to?

Laura. Do not touch me!

Stephen. So — it is he; you follow with the crowd.
Faugh! is there not one byway in the world
But I must find my brother at the end?
Go — you will never reach him. My revenge
Is safe with him.

Laura. I cannot hear nor see you.
My soul is sick with loathing you.

Stephen. Poor fool!
Where have I been these blind and babyish years —
Cringing even to abhorrence! It is over.
Out in the Klondike or the Philippines
I will go find the man in me. Say more,
Brave sister — you alone are wise!

Adela. More — more!
My head aches with it and my heart is sore.

Lois. You have begun — speak now.

Merivale. That we may learn.

Lois. And all the world.

[John Mather, *standing pale and still in his place, has lowered his glass at* Lois's *first word. When* Adela *says, "I have a rôle to play," he slowly, his eyes fixed on* Lois *and hers on him, pours away the wine in it. Then* Lois *faces* Adela *almost buoyantly, and her words, "And all the world" are said with radiant joy.* John *strikes the table, breaking the glass, and addresses the crowd.*

John. 'T is done, our little day,
For greater days have come. Give up its ghost —
Away!

Adela. No, no, for she must speak.

Lois. 'T is true.
We two have still a word ere the day ends.
Give us our sacred hour.

John. Then, shadows all,
Pale maskers, mocking wraiths of gods that were,
Let us go seek the dawn.

Stephen. Where is the dawn?

Merivale. Better the darkness —

Adela. Gather up your rags,
Lest I should strip them off. What do I care
Who shrieks or shivers? Patience has had her day —
Let truth have hers!

Laura. Horrible! horrible!
(*To* Dalton.) Take me away.

Dalton (*to his wife*). If truth must have her day,
Where shall we find it?

Laura. Oh, I am afraid!
Take me away!

[Dalton *gives his hand to* Laura, *and desperately they hasten out.* John *turns to the two men.*

John. Well, is it not enough?

Merivale (*to* Lois). Will you not leave with me this place of storm?
The crowding feet will trample you, the madness
Will pass and leave you cold. Ah, what is life?
A compromise — to win we must concede.
You shall have much, and even this day at last
Shall be forgotten. Come!

Lois. This day is mine —
For all the rest, I know not. It is useless.
My tale is told.

Merivale. I read it to the end,
Here in your face — and shut the book forever.
Steve, the play closes.

Stephen. Leave them to their war.
The hour has struck for you and me. Our war
Is with the fate that struck it, in the day
That dawns.

[*Led by* John, *the three men go out.*

Adela. At last we meet.

Lois. To meet no more.

Adela. I see you as a shadow in my path,
A thing I cannot wound nor crush, that makes
A night around my soul.

Lois. But what of him?
Who cares for you and me?

Adela. Is he not mine—
Mine by the law, mine by his vows?
Lois. Yours—yours!
It would be funny, this fond claim of women—
This mine and thine—if it were not so sad.
Adela. Whose is he then?
Lois. Whose then is everyone?
He is the world's—and God's.
Adela. Not for your pleasure
You try to steal away his soul from me,
But for the world, and God!
Lois. His soul, say you?
I found it on the highway, beaten, robbed,
And left for dead. Should I have passed it by
With all who looked and passed?
Adela. Samaritan!
Then it was charity that brought you here—
Here to my house.
Lois. Ah! have you won the right
To invoke the ancient laws? What long observance
Has made your house a temple? Where is lit
Its altar fire?
Adela. I've done the best I could.
Lois. 'T is not enough then.
Adela. And should he do nothing?

He married me, he pledged his love to me,
And I — poor fool — fancied the tale was over,
And nothing left to tell but happiness.
Alas! the bride-flowers withered in my hands,
Dried up and blew away like dust. My own,
My right, the one thing bound to me, escaped
me.
I am lost in the huge world.

Lois. You held him close
To keep him for yourself who is for all.
Where are the songs you should have bade him
sing,
The sons you should have borne him? You
denied him
Life, that will never be denied.

Adela. Life — life!
Was not the problem difficult enough
Without all these? Must I bear children too
To tease my strength away? I gave him all,
And what he gave was but a residue —
The little left through all the thievish days,
When song and art and business and the world
Had taken their plunder. And for even that
little
The women troop like hounds upon the trail,
And I must watch in silence.

Lois. Did you give?
Give more then. I, who find him in the pit,
See not your gift upon him, and your voice,
Calling, I do not hear.

Adela. He will not take
What I can give, and though I shriek aloud
He hears me not.

Lois. The shriek is your own woe,
The gift a chain.

Adela. And you would bid him break it —
You and this questioning age, which undermines
All that was sure in our unstable world.
Oh, how I hate it all! Hear now my word!
I honor more the creature on the street,
Sinning for lust or greed, than her, the spotless,
Whose delicate dalliance lures the souls of men
And cheats the law. By what fine name soever
You call it, what is this but your desire
Unto my place?

Lois. Is it possible you read
So ill the book of fate?

Adela. Even so I read it.

Lois. Some things are locked away from human hope;
Some things too distant are even for desire.
Look at me! I am one who stands aloof.

If I have strength, ah, take it! courage, use it!
Give him his own! If I was born to love,
With a heart big for life and death and sorrow,
Learn of me, be what I shall never be!
You who have lived, fed upon joy and pain,
Know you the agony of us who starve,
Unrecognized by the strange eyes of God?
Here, like the ruined wreckage on the shore,
I watch the mighty ocean bearing out
Its fleets into the storm. I see the ship
Steered to the rocks — the ship my soul would sail,
And all my futile valor rots away
Into the waste of life.

Adela. It is your choice.
Marry the man who wants you — leave to me
My own.

Lois. Enough of you and me! The need,
The longing and the dreams that meet in him
Are his forever. Happier am I,
Lonely, and free to give him all, than he
Who blindly wove these meshes round his soul.
Speechless, he looks at me with haggard eyes,
And every joy my life has ever known
Runs to his feet in tears. All that I am

Is his — or yours — to serve him, and at last
It will avail.

Adela. Your plight puts mine to shame.
My married love becomes a shabby thing
Beside the heroic purple of your passion.
I was not born to understand his ways,
Dowered with your exquisite sympathy. So be it!
But yet I am his wife. When we are old
We two will smile at the dim thought of you
And make a tale of this.

Lois. Oh, if it be
A tale whose end is joy, I shall be glad
Even in my solitude of life or death.
If you will take my task, give him himself,
Then has my love availed, and I may vanish
Out of your lives forever. Be his wife —
Is it not enough? Give all, and more, and more,
As the warm sun gives to the longing earth.
Then will you make a summer for his soul,
And he will rise on wings into the light,
And I shall be forgotten. Adela,
'Tis my last word to you, and, if you will,
'Tis your last thought of me: take from his life
The need of me.

Adela. I cannot — oh, I cannot!
I am too weak, too selfish, too afraid.
(*She weeps.*)
Why was I born?
Lois. Are you not here — beside him?
You must be strong to do it.
Adela. I have failed.
Better if I could give it up and die.
The past is never over — nevermore
May I begin again.

[John Mather *appears at the doorway.* Adela *observes him and runs out, still passionately weeping.* Lois *turns and sees him, and stands in silence, while he approaches and bows low.*

John. So — it is said.
Lois. You never said it, though — thank you for that.
John. What was the need? Could I not see you knew it?
Lois. I knew it as the clover knows the bee.
When he has flown, how may a poor flower know?
John. You doubted me?
Lois. I doubted my own joy.

John. 'T is joy, then? And I feared to bring you sorrow
By loving you.
Lois. Sorrow! If it be true
There is no longer sorrow in the world.
John. May I be glad then?
Lois. Listen — if to-morrow
This wonder that you tell me is no more —
For it must end —
John. As ends the world —
Lois. Remember —
You need not grieve for me nor think of me.
This hour is mine forever.
John. Share with me!
Is it not ours forever?
Lois. 'T is as though
I died now — you may rightfully forget.
John. And put you in the grave. How cheerfully
You bid me look upon the dark again!
Lois. All — all is yours. Remembering or forgetting,
What difference? If I touch you as I pass —
John. With plumy wings —
Lois. If I but say a word,

Surely my little utmost all is done,
And you may make a song of it.
John. It makes
My life a song.
Lois. Good-by now.
John. Is it this —
Your word?
Lois. Two words, the greatest in the world,
I say to you — I love you, and farewell.
Are they not all?
John. Ah no — for there are deserts
Where you and I would be a world.
Lois. Ah no!
Too bright the sun is there — not to be borne.
It would suffice too much.
John. It would suffice.
Lois. It would consume. If you were born, perhaps,
To conquer, not escape —
John. But here alone —
See, do you find me conquering?
Lois. 'T is done,
Our little day, for greater days are come.
[*She opens the broad screen-door.*
Look, where the storm fell black, now rides the moon.

The thick rain all is over — nothing left
But the rich wetness on the shining leaves,
And all to-morrow's flowers. I do not fear
To leave you.

John. But I fear.

Lois. Ah, where you are
My life is — will you make me live in vain?
Come — to my heart; and kiss me on the lips,
My love, my lover!

[*They embrace.*

John. The great words you said
I say them too — I love you, and farewell.
We shall outrun desire and hope at last,
And find each other somewhere in the light,
When I have done your bidding. 'T is the hour —
Good-by.

Lois. The east grows brave for me. Good-by.

[*She goes out.*

AT THE GOAL

At the Goal

SCENE.—*A bedroom exquisitely furnished with precious old furniture, rugs, and hangings, and softly lit by a night lamp, and a wood-fire burning on the broad hearth. A sick* MAN, *about fifty-five years old, lies in bed motionless, half comatose. A* WOMAN *of fifty, dressed as a nurse in a blue and white striped gown, with broad white collar and long apron, sits looking in the fire. She rises as her patient stirs, and notes the change which comes over him. He opens his eyes, breathes less heavily, and tries to lift himself a little.*

The man. Turn up the lamp. That firelight flickers so,
And shadows clutch at me. For hours and hours
I have been flying—out under the moon;
And in my arms asleep were many children,
The sons and daughters I have never known.

It's queer — that billowy motion of the air —
I almost sang against it in my joy
To hold my sons at last. But then I fell —
Fell back to this. Why did I hear out there
A voice I have not thought of all these years,
And see a face floating beyond the world?
The woman. The time has come.
The man. Why do I talk so much?
"Close-mouthed as Drake," they say of me, but now
Some busy little devil wags my tongue.
The woman. The silent years are speaking.
The man. She was pretty —
That country girl. I kissed her by the pool
Down in the woods. I was a country boy —
A baby! And I vowed to go to town
And work for her, and come and marry her,
And all the usual thing.
The woman. And she believed.
The man. What raptures we get over! Do you know
What it is to come to town?
The woman. Do I not know?
The man. Those black blows of the city on one's heart,
Red-hot between them and the fire. The shock

And agony and fright of it! I felt
Everything change. I died and was reborn
Harder, more keen. The pitiless battering
New-shaped me, and I took the shape and gave
Thanks for the blows that struck a weapon out
Fit for great wars.

The woman. And who should feel its edge
Sooner than she?

The man. She?—oh, that little past
Where she was faded, dwindled, blew away.

The woman. You never took the trouble to strike her dead.

The man. What man could think of woman when the roar
Called him to battle? Inch by inch I crept;
Yes, rank by rank I passed them, while the field
Grew large around me. Men are fighters yet:
In banks and shops and inner offices
We wage the modern war.

The woman. And women still
Think you are lovers.

The man. Love is made for those
Who can get nothing else.

The woman. Who ask naught else.

The man. Love! can love give to me the big round world

To play ball with? What lover's madness ever
Can match that thrill that gathers in the brain
And tingles in these aching finger-tips
As one by one the mighty men go down
And take their orders? Have you ever heard
The little fools who live because we let them
Talk of the vanity of power?
The woman. I prove
Daily the vanity of all things.
The man. Bosh!
Then you have never lived.
The woman. Millions like me
Have never lived because just one like you
Must play ball with the world.
The man. Who moves the world,
The million or the one? Is it my strength,
My single strength — good God! The time is with me,
Whispering, pushing, arming me — a spirit
That will not be denied. What have I done?
Wrecked and remade, torn down and built again
After the brave new plan. Let them beware
Who stand against me, let them rot in sloth
Who do not help me! I have heard the voice —
I care not for their railing.

The woman. Heard the voice;
And won intolerable, unutterable
Wealth by its bidding.
The man. Won the good hard money —
Powder and shot and rations, and the zeal
Of the embattled armies. Money first,
And then the rest for him who dares.
The woman. No matter
What wreckage and what cries.
The man. No matter — no!
A redness at the dawn, a richer soil
For the new harvest.
The woman. 'T is no matter then
Who falls.
The man. Who are you to dispute with me,
As though my youth stood here again, with all
Unanswerable follies in his eyes?
Turn to the light — you with your stripes and apron,
You nurse or prophetess. There is a mist
That hides you, yet — Come closer, give me room.
Who are you?
The woman. One who never lived.
The man. You are —

The woman. I am your past.
The man. And you are here.
The woman. I bring
The lost things.
The man. Let them go!
The woman. They burden me.
I give them back to you.
The man. Intolerable!
The woman. Withered and shrunken, would you know them now —
The lyric joy, the love, the modesty,
The faith; the beauty of the blossoming world —
All June, all sunshine? Would you know them now —
The burden I have carried all these years?
The man. How came you here?
The woman. I have been very patient,
Because I knew that we should meet again.
The man. You knew.
The woman. Fate has denied me other things,
But never that.
The man. I think I must be dying.
I must have tramped the whole big track around

To find you standing like a column there,
Just where I started from.

The woman. Yes — you must die.

The man. To-night?

The woman. Before the dawn.

The man. And all is done —
You have fought for me?

The woman. We fought and we are beaten.
A little vivid hour is yours to think in —
Then all is done.

The man. Death. Now. Lord, what a mess they 'll make of it,
Davis and Chalmers! Call them!

The woman. They are gone.

The man. Damn them! Could they not watch with me an hour?
Write then.

The woman (taking paper and pencil). Go on.

The man. Tell them to wait, keep cool.
Tell them to let Wisconsin fall to nothing,
And get control of it; for we must have it
To strengthen C. and O. Tell them — you hear me? —

The woman. I follow you.

The man. And in that copper deal
They must be smooth and secret, soft as death,

And let that fresh young fool keep up the
game
With his dead father's millions. Blusterer!
He 'll find himself entangled in my nets.
Then they can draw him in without a noise —
Him and his properties.

The woman. Can draw him in —

The man. Tell them to draw the world in,
for this age
Is bigger than the world, and men are born
Who shall own kings — yea, give them peace
or war,
And make the aging earth anew. Alas!
Have I been bold, and wasted not, nor spared,
Stopping at nothing, heaping stone on stone
To build a great colossus, only to leave it
Undone and insecure? Tell them — good
Lord!
They cannot do it. What 's the use of them
When I am gone? Cold wheels without the
fire
To move them. Do not write. Give me the
paper.

[*He tears it to pieces.*

What incoherent fragments death will make
Of all my plans!

The woman. And none will know nor care.
The man. The imbecile, satiric, thankless world
Will go its way without me.
The woman. And forget you.
The man. It shall not. On the gates of hospitals
My name is carved in stone. Millions of mine
Shall build a mighty palace of the arts.
Where I walked flowers will grow.
The woman. The people's treasure —
The spoil of purchased laws and managed markets,
Restored a little after many years.
The man. Bah! Have you naught to say of states enriched,
Deserts made habitable, men employed?
Open your eyes — one mind, even to-day,
May find a world and give it to the race;
And such as you would stop the work with scruples —
Cobwebs no brave man sees.
The woman. And such as I
Would bid the brave man cast away the world
And save his soul.
The man. His soul must take its chance.

The woman. Be honest, then. Give it the truth to carry
Up to the throne of God. Stand by your life,
And drop the hospitals and galleries —
The lies.

The man. The playthings. I who work with fate
Must have immortals for my playfellows.
I love these lovely things. I make them mine.
I rest in them.

The woman. Yours! yours to take and give!
They were not, are not yours — that is the lie.

The man. The lie — the truth! An evenly balanced world
You make of it. The truth — the lie!

The woman. Well?

The man. Well —
There is no absolute — not here.

The woman (looking about). Not here.

The man. The truth, the pure uncompromising truth —
What man would know it?

The woman. Not another hour
Is given to you to turn and face the truth,
Blinding, destroying.

The man. Not another hour —
It is too short.
The woman. It is enough.
The man. Perhaps
If I had married you — there in my youth,
We should have tried to face it.
The woman. Can you feel
That other life?
The man. We might have done great things.
The woman. Together — for the world.
The man. If you had loved me,
It might have been.
The woman. If I had loved!
The man. The truth! —
This is revenge, not love.
The woman. If I had loved —
The man. As woman must who saves her world — the love
Unspeakable, enduring.
The woman. I have sorrowed.
The man. Wept for the renegade, perhaps. My name,
Looming so large of late, has made you dream
Down in your quiet place. But now to-night
You face me with an eye as free as mine.
The glamour all has faded. You are glad.

The woman. You blind and buffet me. I do not know.

The man. Time — time is given you. I who sweat and pant
Wave but a dusty banner as I pass —

The woman. Into the distance.

The man. When the long dark ride
Is over, shall I find you at the goal
Again?

The woman. I have not loved — I do not know.

The man. Wait — I shall look for you.

The woman. We are two braggarts —
Two miserable creatures who have failed.

The man. Then here 's to better luck on the next course!
Shall I go on?

The woman. Is there no more?

The man. Where is she?

The woman. She waits my summons — 't is the modern way.

The man. She fears?

The woman. She weeps and trembles.

The man. Do not call her.
The exquisite, soft, feminine, brilliant thing —
She is for life, not death.

The woman. And I for death.

The man. Take heart. You who have seen so many die —
Live now.

The woman. I who have seen so many die
For the first time see death.

The man. Like a great river
It washes over me.

The woman. Hold fast.

The man. So — So —
Give me your hand. Now I can wait a little.
See — do you smell the clover?

The woman. It is over —
The little vivid hour.

The man. So cool and sweet!
Come to the fields — [*He dies.*

The woman. I cannot! oh, I cannot!

[The woman *throws herself on her knees beside the couch, her arms stretched over the form of* the man. *After a time she slowly rises; closes the eyes, disposes the arms, smooths sheets and pillows, and after a close long look in the face passes out.*

AFTER ALL

After All

SCENE. — *A pathway in hell. On the right snow-drifts, on the left the lake of fire. A few spirits are half visible.*

Chorus of Spirits.

See them coming —
  Flakes that drift,
Ashen mists
  That shift and lift.
Shaken off,
  Ghosts of pain,
Down from earth
  They fall like rain.

Room for the lost! —
  There 's room in hell.
Damned and tossed
  With curse and knell,
Spewed from earth,
  Refused in heaven,

Hail to the lost,
By torments driven!

Lo! who cometh? —
Wise was he.
The last fine secret
He would see.
Alone, aloof
From life and care,
He spun his cobwebs
In the air.

Hush and wonder!
One hath risen
To greet this wisp,
So blanched and wizen:
She who tore
Her soul in two,
Who dared the utmost
Life may do.

[*The spirits of a man and a woman meet.*

She. Ah — you!
He. Yea, I.
She. How did you come?
He. I slipped like sleet adown the wind.
She. You from your heights.

He. The dry years thinned
My soul. It grew too cold and numb
For earth.

She. So high and still you were
I used to think you need not stir
To entér paradise.

He. And now
The dry snow sifts me, and my brow
Chills the dark wind.

She. And I in flame
Bathe my hot wounds away.

He. At last
We who have lost may know the game.

She. Yea, we who missed the fateful cast,
Faltering when the angel passed,
May count his footsteps one by one
Down to our earth, back to his sun.

He. And we who never spake before
May utter pallid words.

She. And we
Whose wind-drawn senses feel no more,
May tell the ruinous heart-throbs o'er
That beat us down this bitter path.

He. We — pale inheritors of wrath,
Who might be treading, hand in hand,
Spaces afoam with wings.

She. If you,
That day when God was with us two,
Had given me the supreme command.
He. If you had stood less proudly there
Against the sun, had seemed aware
Of the desire that did not dare.
She. I who dared all!
He. If the red lips,
That smiled, had trembled once. If even
One quiver of the finger-tips
Had proved you woman —
She. If like a man
You had torn the veil —
He. We blurred God's plan —
Rust on the shining rim of heaven.
Chorus of Spirits.
Come and see them
Cringe and cower —
Fools who missed
The perfect hour!
Dumb and blind,
To them was given
Light, love, joy,
A glimpse of heaven.
In the full day
They lost the way.

Spurn them, laugh at them —
Saints astray!

She. I saw the open gates that morning,
Heard seraph songs.

He. I felt the warning —
From heaven to hell measured the fall.

She. We looked in the archangel's eyes
And dared not follow.

He. We are here.

She. How swiftly fell that black surprise!
I saw you not, and over all
A thick doubt grew, a foggy fear.

He. I turned and made me over-wise
With learning, called the loss of you
By the fond name of sacrifice;
And in my solitudes again
Dreamed I might find the truth for men.

She. And I wandered the dark world through,
Driven by that reckless need of love
Which maddens women.

He. While above
All need I urged my flattered soul.

She. I drank the cup of drunkenness,
And lo, it cursed that could not bless —
Another woman's joy I stole.

He. Yea, when the uproar came to me,
I marveled that such fire could be
In one who seemed so cold.
She. You lit
The fire.
He. If I had nourished it,
Out of my cold philosophy
It would have driven the chill.
She. Ah me!
Then the great fame you made —
He. Will die.
My truth was but another lie.
I had not lived, I could not know.
She. My bliss was but another woe.
Strained to my heart it turned to stone;
And when God bade me let it go
I would not, though it dragged me prone
Down to these fires that melt it not
Where on my breast heavy and hot
It lies.
He. Hush! do you hear the cries
Hurled from the wrath that never dies?
Chorus of Spirits.
In winds of fire and sleet
Whirl on forever!
Never to part nor meet,
Forgetting never.

When the great ghosts wheel down
  Cringe ye and cower!
Who chose the fiery crown
  Shall wield the power.
  Make way! make way! —
  Intruders gray!
Slip through the drear shades
  As ye may!
  Flee in fear!
  Come not near!
Slaves! eternally
  Shift and veer!

He. Warped and twisted and bent are we —
Dried hopes blown down the vales of pain.

She. Hush! do you hear that sound like rain
Of falling souls? Look, do you see?

He. And one with lightning armed?

She. Ah me!
I know him, he has passed me by.

He. Flee from the whirlwind! Dive and fly!

She. Down! down! I hear you not. The gale
Blackens around me.

He. Lo, I fail!

Chorus of Spirits (*approaching*).

Somewhere or other
  The mad world is spinning.
Our game now another
  Gay crowd is beginning.
Ha, ha! they will botch it,
  For God has control.
We nip it and notch it —
  He plays for the whole.

He rumbled and grumbled —
  We would not give ear.
Our power he has humbled
  By pitching us here.
Since heaven is not for us
  And earth 's but a fool —
Since either would bore us
  In hell let us rule!

A MODERN MINUET

A Modern Minuet

SCENE. — *A small room opening into a dancing hall in a modern town house, where a costume party is going on. The room is furnished in eighteenth century style, and a young man and woman, dressed in costumes of Queen Anne's time, are discovered alone. The music of a dance is dimly heard.*

Althea. Ah no, I cannot hear, how dare you tell
Your tale in prose, my lord?
Roderick. Is it not well
To speak the truth, even though a maid be fair
And royally appareled?
Althea. Look, we wear
The Addisonian livery. Let our speech
Ripple with rhymes and flatteries, I beseech.
Why have we slipped the iron leash of time,

Escaped out of the real, save to climb
The trimmed and velvet slopes where maids and men
May play at passion?
Roderick. Let me pledge you then
A flowery love. A garden is my heart,
Planted with rose trees set with formal art
Between green hedges. There you come like spring,
Bidding me bloom while all the sweet birds sing.
Althea. And the red rose half open in its bud —
Is that for me?
Roderick. Take my life's richest blood,
Crimson, deep-scented.
Althea. Lo, the white one there!
Roderick. 'T is my new hope greeting the sunny air.
Breathe gently, lest thou sweep its petals frail
Down the chill wind.
Althea. May a chill wind prevail
In your fair garden?
Roderick. Fickle is the May,
Proud, merciless. Look — if she smiles to-day
To-morrow come the darkness and the storm.
Althea. To-morrow is not, never is. When warm

Shines the sweet sun through the soft sifted air
Who counts the thunders?
Roderick. When the sun shines fair
He who stands tiptoe on the peak of rapture
Thrills with sharp pain because no dream can capture
Another moment so divine.
Althea. Which proves
How foolish 'tis to think. The soul that loves
Tears the pale web of thought, the theories
Whose thick and twisted wisdom once was his
Before the light burst in.
Roderick. The loving soul
Fashions a doubt out of each dream's control,
An agony out of each bliss denied.
Althea. But who can gauge a bliss till it be tried,
Or of the most adventurous dream beware
Till he has leashed it winging in mid-air?
Roderick. Such reckless valor ne'er moved mortal man
As mine were if I dared the space to span
'Twixt me and my desire.
Althea. When man dares not
The gods blot out a planet from the spot
Where it should wheel around some star's bright seat.

Roderick. Ah give me then the universe complete!

[*He falls on one knee and kisses her hand.*

Althea. Nay, nay — beware! Your lady's finger-tip
Takes not the homage of the eye and lip.

Roderick. Set me some task! The sword rusts at my side.
Bid me through dark wars cleave a pathway wide.

Althea. Life is but war — the field awaits the brave.
Rise and go forth to conquer and to save.

Roderick. But ere I rise — a gauge! — lest I return
Spent, wounded, and you know me not, and spurn
The world-worn warrior from your palace gate.

[*She unclasps and hands him a bracelet.*

Althea. Take then this bauble. On my pulse it sate
Counting the heartbeats. Lo, I wait unfriended
Till the brave fight be won, the trial ended.

Roderick (*rising*). And if a century or two should fling
Their spell about us ere once more I bring
This token to your feet, if the bold world

Should down the zones of change be madly
 whirled
Into a dumb and unromantic day,
Then should I find my lady waiting? — say!
Plain words upon her lips, her gown unquilted,
Her hair of nature's gold, her manners wilted
Into a democrat simplicity —
Then would she know me, though my garments
 be
No longer silken, though my head emerge
Out of this snowy coil — yea, though I urge
An homely suit and pledge a workman's hand,
Without the sword in 't? Would she understand
Though all else change, my heart is hers for-
 ever?
 Althea. Ah, if time plods through centuries
 when we sever
'T is but his custom, for whene'er we meet,
After long ages lost and incomplete,
The world seems made anew.
 Roderick. Let it be ours —
That glad new world, its rush of glowing hours!
There let us laugh at time and all the slaves
Who creep through sunless paths into dark
 graves
Blind, unaware of love. Sweet, do you love me?

Althea. Hush! — by the stars that speak the
truth above me,
How dare you strain our airy rhymes and lies
With that great word?
Roderick. Tell me then with your eyes,
Truer than stars. In any way you please
Tell me you love me. Tell me, or I seize
From your shut lips the pledge.
Althea. Would you not scorn
A patched and powdered promise?
Roderick. Hearts are sworn
In every livery, and the pledges spoken
Under a mask are not more lightly broken
Than plain vows clad in rags.
Althea. Ah, give me time —
A century or two whose rush sublime
Shall blast this florid world and make a new one,
Better for simple souls to work and woo on,
Before the sun climbs out of yonder lake.
Roderick. A century or two for your sweet
sake
Is but an hour. Devoutly will I wait,
Your knight kneeling till dawn in lonely state,
Ere from his love he hears the high command
That puts his valor to the proof.
Althea. The band.

Ripples a minuet. Before that change —
That leap of time out of this narrow range,
That sudden sun-burst o'er a world awake —
Shall we not tread a lordly measure, take
A proud farewell of the dear vanities?

Roderick. For that or any walk in life you please,
My hand is yours.

Althea. Come! with your hand in mine,
No road too rough is and no stage too fine.

[*They make the minuet bow and courtesy, and go out hand in hand, taking the minuet step in time to the music.*

IT PASSES BY

PERSONS OF THE PLAY.

Dr. Merrill.
Richard Blake.
Harold Humphrey.

Isabel Everett.
Ellen Rathbourne.
Kate Doane.
Ida Doane.
Phœbe Everett.

It Passes By

SCENE. — *Front drawing-room of a town house facing a broad avenue; a beautiful and home-like room, full of color, furnished with taste and elegance but without great richness. Hexagonal triple window at rear of stage gives to the street. Fireplace with low fire at right; at left, double doorway from the hall, with doors rolled away and portières drawn back. Partly visible through it, at the end of the hall outside, is the front door, giving also to the street down a flight of steps. One or two elms are visible through the windows, their leaves browning and falling under the warm October sunshine; beyond them, across the street, the dim row of houses.*

A little girl of five or six has thrown her doll face downward on a chair, and stands at the window looking out. A handsome woman of about thirty-five, her mother, enters from the hall.

Phœbe. What are they doing, mother?

Isabel (*without noting*). I don't know.

Phœbe. But look — so many people —

Isabel (*searching the tables for something*). Never mind.

Come here, and help me.

Phœbe. Won't they go away?

Isabel. I think so, dear. Where can it be? He had it —

Phœbe. There 's a policeman. Is a circus coming?

Isabel. What are you saying?

Phœbe (*running across and dragging at her mother's skirts*). May I stay and see it?

Look, mother, may I?

Isabel (*following to the window*). What a crowd, my robin!

All down the street — no end to them — I wonder

Why they are here.

Phœbe. Is it a circus then?

And will there be gold chariots?

Isabel (*sitting and lifting the child to her knee*).
Little one,
Mother knows nothing, nothing any more —
Phœbe. But why?
Isabel. All day and night, two days and nights,
Father has suffered so!
Phœbe. Why don't you whisper?
Isabel. My darling must be still again to-day,
Still as a baby birdling in its shell.
And by and by, when something happens there,
Out in the street, she must not run upstairs,
Nor call to mother —
Phœbe. Must I stay alone? —
Here all alone?
Isabel. Dolly is waiting here.
Dolly will play with you.
Phœbe. But she is tired.
Isabel. And all the people and the horses there
To look at —
Phœbe. Who will tell me?
Isabel. And perhaps —
If you watch quietly, some one may come.
Phœbe. Who?

Isabel. Let me think. Perhaps your newest friend —
Your Mr. Blake.

Phœbe. Oh, will he?

Isabel. Or perhaps —
Look there! some one is coming. Do you see?

Phœbe (*springing out of her mother's lap and clapping her hands*). Miss Ellen!

Isabel. Run and welcome her — so softly —
Still as a sunbeam —

[*The child runs and opens the door, admitting* Ellen Rathbourne, *a young woman of twenty-five or twenty-six, who catches her up in her arms.*

Ellen. Darling!

Phœbe. You must whisper —
Father is ill.

Ellen. Isabel, is it true?

Isabel. These two days.

Ellen. Oh, what is it?

Isabel. Pain — pain.

Ellen. You do not fear?

Isabel. No — no! — but it is hard
To see a strong man suffer.

Ellen. Go to him —

Leave her with me. The soldiers, Phœbe mine,
Soon we shall see their banners down the street.
Phœbe. And bands? — and will they march?
Isabel. What is it then —
This crowd?
Ellen. The governor — have you forgot?
This morning the procession passes here.
Isabel. I had forgotten utterly.
Ellen. He goes
In state to his last rest — his first and last.
Isabel. He had his foot upon the White House stair
When the grave opened.
Ellen. Do you think in heaven
He finds the fairest mansion half so fair?
Isabel. He loved the fat old earth.
Ellen. I saw him once —
Isabel. I felt him once — that day he spoke for Grant
In the convention, when the galleries
Went mad with cheers.
Ellen. And now how suddenly —
Isabel. The ladder breaks with him!
Phœbe. I hear a drum.
Ellen. See how they crowd! The yard, the steps —

Phœbe. Look, mother!
I hear a drum.
Isabel. Far, far away, my brown one,
What do you see?
Phœbe. So many people waiting.
Isabel. And something down the street?
Phœbe. It shines like silver.
Isabel. Soldiers, with banners. Watch until it grows
Into an army. Ellen, have you heard —
Tell me before I leave you — have you heard
Richard is here again?
Ellen. Why — yes. But why
The shadow in your voice, my Isabel?
Do you imagine that his name can still
Set my least nerve a-tremble?
Isabel. Oh, I know, —
Yet somehow, so irrational am I,
I catch myself regretting it is over.
Ellen. Well, it *is* over.
Isabel. Years of sun and wind,
Out in that Arizona wilderness,
Have stamped him like a monumental rock
With ruggedness.
Ellen. I laughed at his white hands!

Isabel. And the fierce colors of those arid wastes —
Those deep, eternal, terrifying colors,
Stringing the earth with jewels mountain-high —
He makes me think of them.
Ellen. Colors of death!
So will the earth harden and bake at last,
When we are gone with all our lives and loves.
Why will you talk of dead things? Do those drums
Muffle your thoughts like shrouds?
Isabel. Are you not hard?
Ellen. You married women! tell me why it is
That everything is nothing to you. Queer!
A man may jilt a woman, throw her over
For any base entanglement, and then
The best of you will plead for him.
Isabel. Oh, Ellen —
Do you dare judge by deeds? What a man does
Is accident — so cramped are human lives.
Great souls go blundering on, even to the heights,
While we stand shuddering at the dismal fields
They struggled through and passed.

Ellen. He would not send
A messenger — why do you say these things?
Isabel. For love of you.
Ellen. You do not know me then.
There is no ember of that old fire left.
When chance brings us together we shall meet
Without emotion.
Isabel. If it were to-day?
Ellen. To-day, to-morrow, or beyond the last
Of all the morrows.
Phœbe. See that soldier there,
Riding against the people — will he kill them?
Isabel. I hope not — he 's the marshal making room.
Phœbe. What for?
Ellen. For a great conqueror.
Phœbe. A giant?
Ellen. Yes, one who stalks between us and the sun
With little winks for eyes that see too clear.
Phœbe. I don't like giants.
Ellen. Even when they are kind?
Phœbe. See Mr. Humphrey pushing through the crowd,
And Miss Doane — see them!

Ellen (*waving and smiling out of the window*).
They can scarcely move.
Three more guests, Isabel: they 're coming in,
Or trying to.

Isabel. Then you shall play the hostess.
To-day I cannot see them — I must go.

Ellen. Leave all to me, and do not give a thought
Either to Phœbe, or the invading world.
They shall be mine to-day.

[Isabel *throws her arms about* Ellen's *neck an instant, then goes out at left and runs upstairs.*

Phœbe. But will he come
On horseback?

Ellen. Patience, darling. Who can tell?

The marshal cantered by,
The great drum-major came;
The soldiers too
In coats of blue,
The guns with hearts of flame.

And all the world said — why?
And all the world said — where?
We carry just
A peck of dust
Out to the garden there.

Phœbe. Say it again.

Ellen. Nay, Phœbe, nevermore.

The gilded horseman jumps,
The big policeman thumps,
The people stand like stumps
And will not budge them —
See, they are coming — pushing up the steps,
And you and I must give them the best place
And be polite as princes. Let them in,
And I will bring the chairs —

[Phœbe *runs to the front door again and opens it, admitting* Kate *and* Ida Doane, *and* Harold Humphrey. Ellen *brings chairs to the windows, humming in time to the drums.*

We carry just
A peck of dust
Out to the garden there.
Here — take the box.
One moment, and we ring the curtain up.

Kate. These holidays! what can you do with them?
I meant to hide from this, take refuge in
Some innocent excitement — hemming sheets,
Playing the mandolin, or reading through
That artless tale of Mrs. Ward's. But no —

This youth was so unutterably bored
By one day's exile from the daily grind,
He vowed to spend the morning, stay to luncheon,
And otherwise afflict us. It was then
I grasped at this procession, and was saved
To share him with you.

Harold. She can tell the truth
Well — once a year at least. Of course you know
How shrewd are her devices to conceal
The sweet affection that she cannot choose
But give me.

Kate. Whose affection?

Harold. On my soul
I have forgotten, though there was a time
When pity made me weep to think of it.

Kate. Your only tear, and may she never know?

Ida. They will talk nonsense, even at funerals.
Phœbe and I are honest; we are here
To see the show. We shall not miss a flag.

Phœbe. But no one tells me.

Ellen (*grandiloquently*). Now the beat of drum
Rhymes with the tramp of armies. Row on row

The gleaming cohorts, like a summer sea,
Roll on in waves that sparkle to the sun.
Now the furled flag, the sad obsequious dirge,
The muzzled guns, mighty with memories,
Bear to its port a life. Look, ere 't is gone.
Interpret, lest it glide into the past
Unheralded.

[*The drums are passing the house, rolling a slow and solemn march at the head of the procession. Soon they grow slowly fainter.*

Kate. A prologue to this play!

Ellen. A prologue, Harold of the ready tongue.

This bark, that dims beyond our narrow verge,
What was it when it rode the swelling seas
And took the gales with joy?

Harold. What was it not?
A shifty ship, built to be serviceable
In any kind of traffic. Once a coaster,
That hugged the shore of politics, nor dared
Venture beyond three fathoms lest it sink.
A transport then, carrying back and forth
Opinions, purposes, adapted to
The popular demand, and sold so cheap
No man need care if they were worn a day
And thrown away the next. A privateer,

That took the chance of war to make a show
And win the prize of glory. Then, grown bold,
A slaver next, dealing in gangs of voters,
Chained, labeled for delivery at the polls,
Ready-made freemen. Last, perhaps a pirate,
Slashing for power, be the flag friend or foe,
And winning it, only to fall at last
There within sight of golden pinnacles —
The city of his dream.

[*In speaking*, Harold *advances from the window.* Ellen *follows.*

Ellen. If this is all
Why did the people love him?

Harold. Blank the people!
Why are the people fools?

Ellen. If this is all
Why do we bow when he goes by to-day,
And feel a sudden dimness at the eyes
To see death beating him?

[*She sinks into an arm-chair standing with its back toward the hall and window.*

Harold. I cannot tell.
The feminine mind should never roam at large
To shift the planets from their courses.

Ellen. Yet
Why are you here if this is all?

Harold. Compulsion,
And a deep joy in dirges.
Phœbe. See the flag!
Why don't they let it wave?
Harold (*returning to the window*). Precisely — why?
Why do they furl it up in crape, I wonder,
When you and I would rather see it float?
Phœbe. Listen! (*A pause.*) It 's solemn, is n't it?

[Kate *suddenly looks frightened and rises from the window-seat, signing to* Ida *for silence. She takes* Harold *by the arm and quietly leads him to front of stage.* Ellen *remains in her chair, her head in her hand — dreaming.*

Kate. Good heavens!
What shall we do?
Harold. Don't scare a man to death!
Do about what?
Kate. Did n't you see him?
Harold. Whom?
Kate. Why, Richard Blake.
Harold. What, back again?
Kate. Oh yes —
Two days ago — but coming in —

Harold. Why not?
Kate. Have you forgotten how he went away?
Harold. What do you mean?
Kate. Oh, give away your brains
If you can't use them! You forget already
That he and Ellen Rathbourne were engaged
Five or six years ago, that he forsook her
For some low creature, and when that was over
Fled to the wilds?
Harold. Oh yes, I do remember.
Kate. Indeed! Well — think again. What shall we do?
Harold. Do nothing.
Kate. But she has not seen him since.
He will come in — she should be spared —
Harold. Oh, pshaw!
She has to meet him sometime — why not now?
Now — to the sound of dirges, and the tramp
Of fate's inexorable armies? — Hush!
Now is the time. Don't interfere with chance,
Who has her plans, deeper than yours or mine.
If we are summoned here as witnesses
Be grateful in all humbleness.
Kate. I own
The pride of sex. If she should pale before him,

So much as tremble, all the woman in me
Would feel defeated.

Harold. Put her to the test —
Else there 's no triumph.

Phœbe (at the window). There 's the doctor coming.
I 'll let him in.

[*She runs to the door.*

Harold. Besides, it is too late.

[Ellen *rises from her revery, throwing her arms up wide and her head back; and turns slowly toward the door.* Kate *and* Harold *turn and face the door.* Ida *stands quietly at the window. Enter* Dr. Merrill, *a man of fifty, and* Richard Blake, *about thirty, of powerful athletic build, his fair skin bronzed by exposure.* Richard *shows the least possible trace of emotion at seeing* Ellen. *The* Doctor, *a few feet in advance, extends his hand to* Ellen, *who greets him first with perfect aplomb. No one seems embarrassed.* Harold *and* Kate *go toward the hall to meet* Richard, *as he stands, hat in hand, beside the portière. The drums sound faint in the distance, to the north — left.*

Ellen. Good morning, Doctor. Your benignant smile
Shines on the just and unjust, like the sun.
You bring a rover with you. Mr. Blake,
You and the sun are comrades.

Kate (*to* Harold). Look at her!
She does it well.

[Ellen *extends her hand to* Richard *indifferently, and he takes it an instant, bowing low in silence.*

Harold. Of course she does. (*To* Richard.) It's good
To see you here again. How is the West?
You wear its colors bravely. You have changed.
What is the city like after these years?

Richard. An orchestra, playing a banging tune
Into incredible silence.

Kate. Music then?

Richard. Intricate harmonies — my ear has lost
The clue.

Ellen (*to the* Doctor). Your patient, is it serious?

Dr. M. (*taking off his overcoat*). A little troublesome, but not alarming.

These youngsters trust this Indian summer day,
But I must put my faith in coats. The hostess?

Ellen. You are the only guest she sees to-day.

Dr. Merrill. Who entertains the world. Look at that stoop!
If this young athlete had not struck for me
I should be digging yet.

Ellen. Such patient crowds!

Dr. M. A mighty funeral!

Kate. Is it not a pity
He could not live to see it?

Harold. The last act
Of a long gaudy melodrama.

Dr. M. Listen!
How easily does youth dispose of him,
Who played so large a rôle! At least admit
He took the stage and held it, even dared
Try to be president.

Harold. Yes, died of scheming.

Dr. M. At any rate he did things. Come, confess —
How long since you have voted?

Harold. I refuse
To chronicle my virtues to the shame
Of this most blatant politician.

Dr. M. Then —
Tell me — whom shall we nominate next June
Instead of him?
Harold. Some farmer from the plough,
Or you, or me, or yonder officer,
Who rides so like a turkey.
Dr. M. It will be
Strange not to hear his voice or shout his name.
The galleries will miss him.
Harold. Yes, their hero.
Dr. M. Well, there is work to do even now. I leave
With you his reputation.
[*The* Doctor, *who has been retreating toward the door, followed by* Kate *and* Harold, *now goes out and upstairs.* Richard *approaches* Ellen, *whom* Phœbe *is trying to drag to the window, and speaks to her, quite indifferent as to whether the others hear him or not. A brass band, playing a dirge, begins to be audible in the distance from the south.*
Richard. I have come
Three thousand miles to have a talk with you.
I am persuaded you will not refuse.

Five years of thinking make me sure at last
That it is right to see you.

Ellen. I will hear
What you may say, though you mistake, I think,
To be so sure.

Richard. Tell me the place — the time.

Ellen. It must be here and now.

Harold (*aside to* Kate — *looking at* Richard).
Look at them now!

Kate (*smiling*). Don't you think we can see better outdoors?
Such a fine dirge is coming, and beyond
The regulars — the guns!

Harold. Yes, let us join
The brave unwashed, beg them for standing-room,
And be good socialists.

[*Exeunt* Harold *and* Kate, *to the front steps.* Ida *rises from the window seat.*

Phœbe. May I go too?
Miss Ellen, may I?

Ellen. Go take care of them.

[Phœbe *pirouettes gleefully, seizes* Ida *by the hand, and they go out. They, the crowded steps, the street, etc., are remotely visible through the open door.*

Richard. Well — after all it is a little thing
I have to tell you, and it matters not
Where it is spoken. It is due to you,
Whom I so greatly wronged, that I should say
You are the only woman in the world
For me, and will be always.

Ellen. Do you think
I value your regard?

Richard. No, not to-day,
Nor can you yet believe in it. Perhaps
You will not ever. Yet it is the truth,
And such small reparation as may lie
In such a truth I offer you.

Ellen. In time
I may have faith in you again, but now
This seems an insult.

Richard. Leave it then to time,
Or else forget it. I am going back —
Back to the desert. There is one thing more
That should be said, and yet I know not how
To say it. You are strong; you have no fear,
Nor any need of service. If life hurts —
You will close with it and conquer. Yet at last,
Some day when you are weary of your strength,
When all the hour fails, and the past alone
Looks fair and sure, you may be willing then

To think of me as longing for a chance
To serve you, even the slightest; you may speak
Thus to your heart: This man, to whom I gave
My first young foolish ardor, he who vowed
To love me always and betrayed the vow,
It seems that he has kept it after all
And somewhere on the earth he lives for me.

Ellen. How strange! — to see you there, to hear your voice
Uttering promises, just as of old,
And yet to feel no faith! I did not know
The past lay dead so deep that you, even you,
Would seem a ghost to me.

[*The music of the dirge grows louder in the street.*

Richard. And yet to me
It is the only thing alive. For me
The summer blooms there always, and the storm
That wrecked it once has faded into light.
I cannot tell how lovely is the place,
How rich, how still.

Ellen. The light that never was!

Richard. It is the garden of my life. To you
Whatever fruits may grow!

Ellen. Will it be sweet —
The fruit of dead hopes and corrupted lives?
Why do you lead me toward the place of death
I fled from long ago?
Richard. But it is gone.
Life out of death, bloom out of decay —
So runs the law. Alone there on the plains,
By night and day, under the sun and stars,
The law has driven me — the offended law,
Armed with its vengeance. And I fled — fled
— fled —
Afraid to look. Gaunt summer buried me
Deep in dry storms, the livid winter rode
Stiff at my side, and still I was afraid.
Still I could hear the clatter and the cry
Behind me. Well — at last I clutched my fear
And turned. Behold, the thing that followed
me
Was love. How strangely beautiful it was —
Austere and fair! A stillness grew around me.
Then the vast world came close, the mighty hills
Drew near and clasped me, even the bright
white moon
Laid her cool hand upon me. And I knew
The sorrow all had vanished, and the joy
Would stay with me.

Ellen. When one may be alone
Perhaps 't is easy to remember.
Richard. You —
You have forgotten?
Ellen. I have waked.
Richard. It passed
And left no bitterness?
Ellen. How can I tell?
The dream just vanished and the truth was there.
And, after all, the truth is best perhaps.
I owe you thanks for knowledge.
Richard. Once I feared
Your faith — so luminous it was, so tempting
To the black winds. And afterwards I feared
The shadow there. I took the shock for you,
And felt a darkness falling. Since the change,
Since my great night, but one desire has held me —
To reach you through the silence. But it seemed
So far! The stars are awful in that south —
Unwinking eyes of the great noiseless God,
Conscious, inscrutable. I watched them shine
Through the keen vivid blue, until it seemed
Much nearer to the stars than to your feet.
Ellen. Yes — I was far away.

Richard. Alone in crowds
As I upon the desert.
Ellen. But it passed.
Richard. I could not come.
Ellen. I could not hear.
Richard. But now
After the years of longing, suddenly
The spacious earth consented — all its wastes
Of sand and sage ; and the high spheric sky,
Even to its verge of suns invisible,
Consented, and I came.
Ellen. How strange it is —
Incredible — that all is just the same,
You here, and I, and yet the love is gone!
Richard. Not strange.
Ellen. Did not I call it by large names?
Eternal and unchangeable it was,
Fate ordered it, God sanctioned it, our souls
Were one for life and death.
Richard. For life and death.
Ellen. I have never been so sure of anything,
Never so sure. And yet to-day perhaps
This festival of death is made for that,
And the long dirges mourn it.

Richard. Peace be with it! —
And honor!

Ellen. Peace and honor! It becomes
A happy memory which has been a shame.
Now I may light white candles on that altar,
Set lilies there.

Richard. I bring them, and from me
You take them. Look! I thank you from my soul.

[*He takes her hands, and they look in each other's eyes a moment.*

Ellen. Why did my lover leave me?

Richard. Oh, your eyes
Conjure these desolate years away!

[*He drops her hands and turns away.*

Ellen. *You* left me.

Richard. Ask it of him — the scholar, general,
President almost.

Ellen. Unto Cæsar then
You dare appeal.

Richard. To Cæsar!

Ellen. Hush — he pays
The forfeit.

[*The dirge is passing the house. Soon it begins to grow slowly fainter.*

Richard. Lavishly we lay all down —
Ellen. Why? Why?
Richard. There is a beast that drives us on,
And a dark riddle waiting in the pit.
Ellen. And in the pit you do not spare the lost —
The riddle who is woman.
Richard. Once she was,
Ages ago, before such brutes as I
Made her a devil. The score is old between us —
Eternity will strike the balance there.
Ellen. And I was singing up those mapled hills
A thousand miles away — and dreaming dreams.
I should have stayed.
Richard. No — no, I was not fit.
Undisciplined, unguided, all my life
The slave of impulse — no, it was to be,
Must be, to save us.
Ellen. Though we died of it.
Richard. I saw you lying white, in a scorched world.
Ellen. I learned to be alone, and not afraid.
Richard. I saw you always — so the courage came.

My life had been a garden made for me;
Now it should be a desert. I would gnaw
The rocks for sustenance, winnow my will
Through whirling sand-storms. I would take from men
Nothing, from fortune nothing. I would give
The leaping beast in me a bitter fight —

Ellen. Hush! — I grow dizzy. Let me think! — So you —
The traitor and deserter, whom I swept
Out of my life — you are the faithful lover,
And I the faithless.

Richard. You were brave.

Ellen. But now —
Now you are here, a man, a conqueror —
Oh yes, I see the battle in your face,
The victory in your eyes — now you are here,
Why do I fail?

Richard. Good God! it is not you!

Ellen. Have I grown hard while you were growing great;
Self-righteous, while that fight for life or death
Taught you humility? I must have lost
Some fineness of the soul that once was mine,
Or I could take your hand and go with you
Up to the mountains.

Richard. Hush!

Ellen. The saddest thing
Is change. I thought I could not live; and then,
When death refused me, knew I could not smile
Ever again. And then — I am ashamed
To tell how soon my life bloomed out again,
And all the past of ecstasy and pain
Was utterly gone, as it had never been.

Richard. The only thing that passes not.

Ellen. I wondered
If anything endured, if human souls
Forgot their seasons like the trees; I dared not
Measure the perfidy. And even to-day.
It frightens me to feel, deep in my heart,
The quest of love, to search the eyes of men —
Each casual new one — with that secret hope.
Oh, you despise me!

[*She sinks into a chair, burying her face in her hands. The dirge in the distance comes to an end and stops.*

Richard. Nothing can forget.
Each summer leaves the record of its growth
Even in the tree. So you have won from me
The power of greater love.

Ellen. Is it not shame —
This eagerness that will not rest from seeking,

That conjures dreams to feed on, seals my heart
Lest lips and eyes betray it? What are we
More than the beasts, if every sense allures us,
And nothing steadfast proves the ruling soul?
And what am I more than that other woman,
Save for the casual fate which cast me here,
And her upon the street?

Richard (*seizing her wrists*). Be still! Good Heaven!
How ignorantly —

Ellen. I have shocked you — so —
Forget me now — you know me as I am.
I never dared confess it to myself.

Richard. The quest of love, you call it. You are blind —
It is the quest of God. You will not find
The starry soul that you are looking for,
Even at the marriage altar. But at last
This violent tumult of the blood will still
Into a deep serenity, and then
The big round world with all its throng of souls
Will be too little for your love.

Ellen (*looking up at him*). Perhaps
I shall no longer feel ashamed, my friend,
Now I have told.

Richard. Shame is a deadly thing —
A curtain at the windows of the soul.

Ellen. I will begin to learn — I have begun.
For knowledge is the thing — I thought that out —
To save us from ourselves. Do we not need it —
We women whom long ages have shut up
With mad emotions? It is sweet to feel
The cool white hand of knowledge on my brow
And bid her lead me toward the far-off light.
Perhaps at last —

Richard. At last —

Ellen. I may be fit
To do some work in the world.

Richard. And all those years
The thought of you will be my gladness.

Ellen. Strange!
Shall I learn to be glad in all those years?

[Phœbe *comes tripping in.*

Phœbe. Miss Ellen, you 're not looking.

[Ellen *turns suddenly and catches the child up with a passionate embrace.*

Ellen. But we will.

Phœbe. It 's coming — Mr. Humphrey says it is —

With six black horses, and a lot of men
Singing a song.

Ellen. And will you show it to us ?

Phœbe. It's big and black, with feathers waving on it.
It's coming next — and these are the Hussars.

[*They approach the windows.*

Ellen. Splendid ! — see how their horses shine and prance !

Phœbe. Why do you stay in here ?

Richard. Because we see
Things even more wonderful. Have you not heard
She is a princess ?

Phœbe. Who ?

Richard. Miss Ellen is —
A princess with a wand. She has a throne
Up in the mountains.

Phœbe. Will she sit upon it ?

Richard (*sitting down and taking* Phœbe *on his knee*). A throne made of new gold, with draperies
Torn down from flaming worlds — purple and yellow,
Queer blues that burn like scarlet, till the sun
Boils over, streaks the whole round polished sky

With orange and hot green, and slowly then
Simmers away. The night comes sailing softly
Above her throne, and cools the ashen air
Into a vast clear fathomless white blue
That shows the stars to her — such flashing stars —
Each one a soul that sings.

Phœbe. And is it far?

Richard. As far as heaven, perhaps.

Ellen. Further than death.

Phœbe. I saw a princess once. She had a star
Lit on her forehead.

[*To the south — right — a dirge begins, chanted by men's voices, with long pauses between strophes. During the first stanza,* Isabel *comes down the stair, followed by the* Doctor. Isabel *pauses at the door an instant, looking with keen anxiety and hope at the three seated unobservant in the window. The next instant* Phœbe *runs to her mother, followed by* Richard.

(*Song without.*)

Soldier, ruler, hero, friend —
In thy train once more we wend.
Lead us onward to the end.

Phœbe. Mother, come and look!
Isabel. Ah, Richard!
Richard. Dear my lady!
[*He takes her hand and bends over it.* Kate, Ida, *and* Harold *enter behind her from the steps.*
Isabel. It is good
To win you from the desert, to expect
Your shadow at my door.
Richard. But I have come
To say good-by.
Isabel. No — no — you shall not say it.
[*She glances beyond at* Ellen, *who at* Richard's *word had turned to look out.*
Harold (*to* Kate). She has a heart, you say.
Kate. If she has not —
Harold. Ah, Mrs. Everett, to you at last
Our homage!
Isabel. Did the other guests make way?
Kate. They all stood up, like silent sentinels,
And then, when we besought, they all sat down.
And so, row upon row, we gazed at ease.
Harold. They were so still that even my eloquent tongue
Caught the disease.
The Doctor. Keep it a moment more.

(*Song without.*)

Life was lavish, life was bold.
Now her blows and boons are told,
Now her dreams thine eyes behold.

Harold. Nay, but not all her dreams!
The Doctor. Now verily
Doth the old order change, since he can die.
Isabel. How vast the infinite must seem to him
Who was so busy in his little world!
Richard. He took its error frankly with its good,
Lived on the level of his time.
Harold. Perhaps,
But not above it.
Ellen. Not a prophet — but —
Harold. A type, an average.
Ellen. And something more —
A man.
Isabel. And with a heart!
The Doctor. And something more —
A leader.
Isabel. Publicly and privately
He erred — and yet —
Richard. We bow to let him pass.

Phœbe (*clapping her hands — at the window*). It's here!

[*All stand silent with bowed heads. The chant grows loud without.*

On the highway fared thy feet,
Marching ever, brave and fleet,
Through the wind, the dust, the heat.

Phœbe (*looking up at* Richard). Why do they sing? Is it for God?

[Harold *smiles, and some of the others.* Richard *stoops and lifts her.*

Richard. For God, or else how could he know?

Ellen. Ah, Phœbe!

The Doctor. So he is gone!

Harold. And we must go.

Isabel. And I —
Back to the sick.

Harold. I to the office.

Kate. I —
To — which, of half an hundred things that claim me?

Harold (*to* Richard). And you — what is it calls you from the West?

Richard. Dry wastes, that thirst for rivers.

Harold. You will reap
Harvests, where never blade of grass has grown.
Ellen. The wilderness will sing for you.
Richard. And you —
Ellen. Oh, let me learn!
Phœbe. Is it all over now?
[*The chant is heard more faintly.*
Comes the long sweet solemn night.
Sleep and silence close the fight.
Hush — till morn reveals the right.

THE END.

The Riverside Press
Electrotyped and printed by H. O. Houghton & Co.
Cambridge, Mass., U. S. A.

24 May 2018
Chestertown, Maryland

Dear Chloe,

It's a fine accomplishment to have the quality of your high school work rewarded with admission to an outstanding university. Congratulations!

Enclosed is a small gift that has connections with the Sommers side of your family as well as with your talents in drama.

Harriet Monroe (whose mother was sister to Carol's great-grandfather Richard Mortimer Mitchell) was a famous poet and a central figure in Twentieth Century poetry. There is a bio of her on Wikipedia. You may find something of interest in this volume of verse plays, one of her many published writings.

The wedding of my granddaughter Gwyneth will be on July 1st in Virginia Beach, so I will not be able to accept the invitation to your graduation celebration. This is very disappointing but I hope I may get to see you another time and get acquainted.

My best wishes for a stimulating college experience,

CPSIA information can be obtained
at www.ICGtesting.com
Printed in the USA
BVHW03s1256210518
516898BV00006B/50/P

9 780649 501786